States
IDAHO

by Angie Swanson

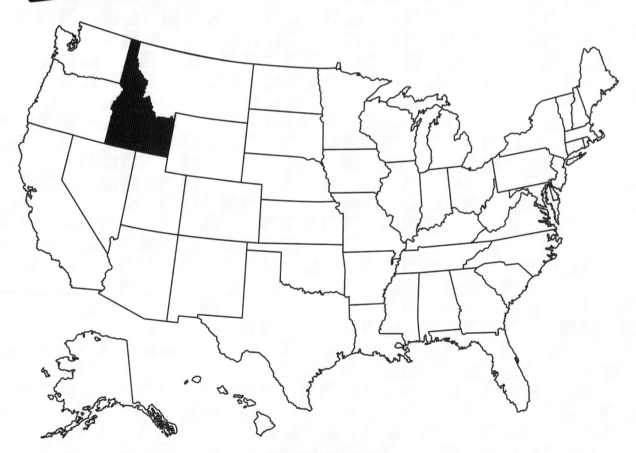

CAPSTONE PRESS
a capstone imprint

Next Page Books are published by Capstone Press,
1710 Roe Crest Drive, North Mankato, Minnesota 56003
www.mycapstone.com

Library of Congress Cataloging-in-Publication Data
Cataloging-in-publication information is on file with the Library of
Congress.
ISBN 978-1-5157-0398-3 (library binding)
ISBN 978-1-5157-0458-4 (paperback)
ISBN 978-1-5157-0510-9 (ebook PDF)

Editorial Credits
Jaclyn Jaycox, editor; Kazuko Collins and Katy LaVigne, designers;
Morgan Walters, media researcher; Laura Manthe, production specialist

Photo Credits
Capstone Press: Angi Gahler, map 4, 7; CriaImages.com: Jay Robert
Nash Collection, top 19; Getty Images: Ed Vebell, 25, Stock Montage,
middle 19; Library of Congress: Library of Congress Prints and
Photographs Division Washington, D.C, 26, 27; Minden Pictures:
Martin Withers, top left 20; Newscom: akg-images, middle 18, David
R. Frazier /DanitaDelimont.com "Danita Delimont Photography",
9, Scott J. Ferrell/Congressional Quarterly, 29, TSN/Icon SMI 800/
TSN/Icon SM, top 18; One Mile Up, Inc., flag, seal 23; Shutterstock:
AVprophoto, top 24, B Brown, bottom left 8, BluIz60, bottom right 20,
Charles Knowles, 5, Everett Historical, 12, 28, Helga Esteb, bottom 18,
IDAK, bottom right 8, 15, Jason Patrick Ross, bottom left 21, jdwfoto,
bottom 19, Jeffrey T. Kreulen, 6, Joseph Sohm, 13, 14, krasky, top
left 21, Makarova Viktoria, middle left 21, Matt Jeppson, middle right
21, Menna, bottom right 21, Peter Kunasz, 10, photowind, top right
20, Png Studio Photography, cover, Radek Svehla, bottom 24, Steve
Lagreca, 7, Tom Reichner, bottom left 20, Tucker James, 11, txking, 17,
Wollertz, 16; Wikimedia: National Park Service, top right 21

All design elements by Shutterstock

Printed and bound in China.
0316/CA21600187
012016   009436F16

TABLE OF CONTENTS

Want to take your research further? Ask your librarian if your school subscribes to PebbleGo Next. If so, when you see this helpful symbol throughout the book, log onto www.pebblegonext.com for bonus downloads and information.

LOCATION

Idaho is in the northwest part of the United States. It's sometimes considered part of the Pacific Northwest. Northern Idaho borders Canada. To the west are the states of Washington and Oregon. Nevada and Utah lie to the south. On the east are Montana and Wyoming. Boise is Idaho's capital and biggest city. It is in southwestern Idaho along the Boise River. Idaho's other large cities are Nampa, Meridian, Idaho Falls, and Pocatello.

PebbleGo Next Bonus! To print and label your own map, go to www.pebblegonext.com and search keywords:

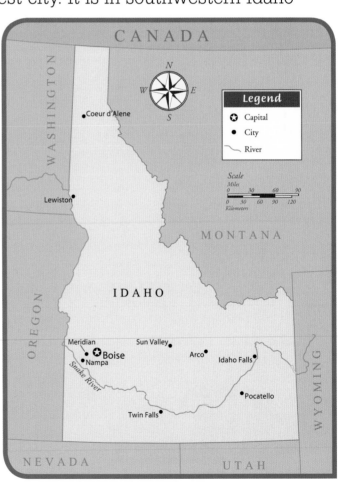

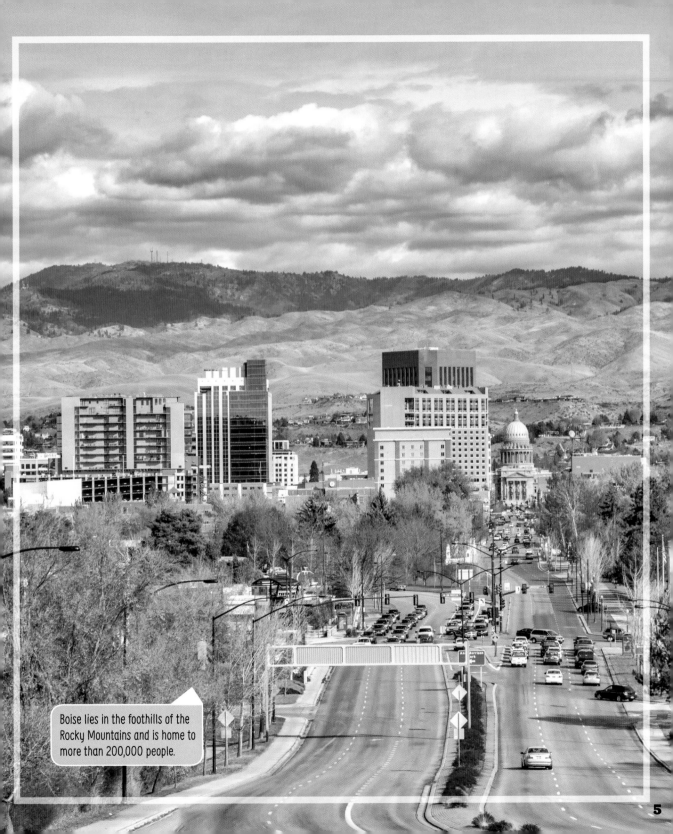

Boise lies in the foothills of the Rocky Mountains and is home to more than 200,000 people.

GEOGRAPHY

Idaho's landscape is filled with mountains, forests, rivers, and lakes. Mountains make up most of the northern part of Idaho. The southern part of Idaho flattens out into the Snake River Plain. The Snake River runs through the Snake River Plain. Idaho has several national and state forests and more than 2,000 lakes. Lake Pend Oreille is Idaho's largest lake. It covers 180 square miles (466 square kilometers). Idaho's highest point is Borah Peak, found in central Idaho. It stands 12,662 feet (3,859 meters) above sea level.

PebbleGo Next Bonus! To watch a video about attractions in each region of Idaho, go to www.pebblegonext.com and search keywords:

ID VIDEO

The large Lake Pend Oreille is also one of the deepest lakes in the United States.

Map Legend

Legend

- ▲ Highest Point
- Lake
- Mountain Range
- ○ Point of Interest
- River

Lake Pend Oreille

BITTERROOT RANGE

Scale
Miles
0   30   60   90
0 30 60 90 120
Kilometers

Salmon River

SALMON RIVER MOUNTAINS

SAWTOOTH RANGE

Borah Peak

Little Lost River

Big Lost River

Snake River

Craters of the Moon National Monument

American Falls Reservoir

Located in the central part of Idaho, Sawtooth National Recreation Area consists of 756,000 acres (305,942 hectares) of mountain country.

WEATHER

Idaho's climate varies. The high mountains get the coldest weather. Southwest Idaho gets the warmest summer weather. The average January temperature is 23 degrees Fahrenheit (minus 5 degrees Celsius). The average July temperature is 67°F (19°C).

Average High and Low Temperatures (Boise, ID)

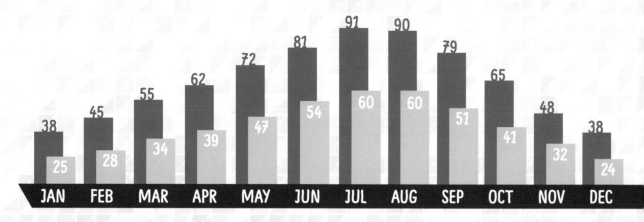

	JAN	FEB	MAR	APR	MAY	JUN	JUL	AUG	SEP	OCT	NOV	DEC
High	38	45	55	62	72	81	91	90	79	65	48	38
Low	25	28	34	39	47	54	60	60	51	41	32	24

LANDMARKS

Nez Perce National Historical Park

Nez Perce National Historical Park spreads across four states. Idaho's park center is in Spalding in the northwestern part of the state. Visitors can view movies and museum exhibits about Nez Perce history and culture. As they tour the site, visitors will also see burial grounds and battlefields.

Shoshone Falls

Shoshone Falls is the largest waterfall on the Snake River. Located near the city of Twin Falls, Shoshone Falls is higher than Niagara Falls. The water plunges 212 feet (65 m) over the steep rock ledges.

Craters of the Moon National Monument

Craters of the Moon National Monument is in central Idaho. This giant lava field came from volcanoes that erupted about 15,000 years ago. Visitors see different types of lava and volcanic cones. They also can walk through long, narrow caves called lava tubes. The caves are made of hardened lava.

Meriwether Lewis (left) and William Clark (right) are famous for exploring the West, including the Idaho area.

People have lived in Idaho for thousands of years. Descendants of those first people formed several American Indian tribes. The two largest groups were the Nez Perce and Shoshone. In 1803 President Thomas Jefferson bought the Louisiana Territory, including present-day Idaho, from France. The sale was called the Louisiana Purchase. In 1805 explorers Meriwether Lewis and William Clark became the first white people to explore the Idaho area. Idaho Territory was created in 1863. Idaho became a state on July 3, 1890.

Idaho's state government is made up of three branches. The governor is the leader of the executive branch, which carries out laws. The legislature is made up of the 35-member Senate and the 70-member House of Representatives. They make the laws for Idaho. Judges and their courts make up the judicial branch. They uphold the laws.

The dome of Idaho's capitol rises 208 feet (63 m) into Boise's skyline.

INDUSTRY

Idaho's economy relies greatly on agriculture, manufacturing, and tourism. Idaho potatoes are known around the world. Idaho farmers also raise wheat, barley, vegetables, and sugar beets. Livestock makes up about 50 percent of Idaho's agricultural income. Sheep and cattle ranching have long been important parts of Idaho's economy.

Manufacturing is Idaho's major industry. Computer equipment and other electronics are the top factory goods. One of the world's largest wood product companies, Boise Cascade, is based in Boise. Boise Cascade produces lumber and paper products. Idahoans also produce sheet metal, rubber, plastic, machinery, and prefabricated houses.

Logs are lifted from a truck during the milling process at a Boise Cascade paper mill.

Tourism is an important industry in Idaho. It is one of the state's many service industries. Millions of tourists visit Idaho every year for its ski resorts and beautiful scenery.

Idaho is popular for its ski resorts, such as this one located in Boise.

POPULATION

Most of Idaho's population is white. Some of these people can trace their ancestry to Idaho's early settlers who arrived in the 1800s. White Idahoans came from different European groups. English, Swedish, German, and Danish ancestry is common. American Indians have always been an important part of Idaho. They include members of the Nez Perce, Kootenai, Coeur d'Alene, Shoshone-Bannock, and Shoshone-Paiute tribes. Boise has the country's largest group of people of Basque ancestry. The Basque are a native people of the Pyrenees Mountains, located between France and Spain.

Population by Ethnicity

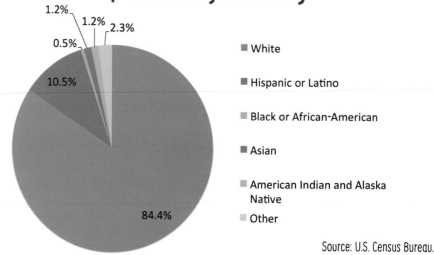

- 1.2%
- 1.2%
- 2.3%
- 0.5%
- 10.5%
- 84.4%

- ■ White
- ■ Hispanic or Latino
- ■ Black or African-American
- ■ Asian
- ■ American Indian and Alaska Native
- ■ Other

Source: U.S. Census Bureau.

Many other Idahoans are of Mexican ancestry. More than 175,000 Hispanics live in the state. Less than 2 percent of Idaho's residents are Asian. African-Americans make up less than 1 percent of Idaho's population.

Over 1.5 million people call Idaho home.

STATE SYMBOLS

Tree

western white pine

Flower

syringa

Bird

mountain bluebird

Dance

square dance

PebbleGo Next Bonus! To make a dessert using Idaho's state vegetable, go to www.pebblegonext.com and search keywords:

ID RECIPE

Fruit

huckleberry

Fossil

Hagerman horse fossil

Horse

appaloosa

Fish

cutthroat trout

Insect

monarch butterfly

Vegetable

potato

21

FAST FACTS

STATEHOOD
1890

CAPITAL ☆
Boise

LARGEST CITY •
Boise

SIZE
82,643 square miles (214,044 sq km) land area (2010 U.S. Census Bureau)

POPULATION
1,612,136 (2013 U.S. Census estimate)

STATE NICKNAME
Gem State

STATE MOTTO
"Esto Perpetua," which is Latin for "Let it be perpetual"

STATE SEAL

The Idaho state seal was officially adopted in 1891. The seal shows the major industries of Idaho. The miner on the right reflects that mining was once the leading industry in Idaho. The woman on the left represents equality and justice. The seal has images that reflect the natural beauty of the state. A mountain stream and a white pine are featured on a shield in the center of the seal. The elk's head above the shield shows Idaho's concern for wildlife. A banner at the top of the seal is printed with the state motto, "Esto Perpetua," which is Latin for "Let it be perpetual."

PebbleGo Next Bonus!
To print and color
your own flag, go to
www.pebblegonext.com
and search keywords:

ID FLAG

STATE FLAG

Idaho's state flag features the state seal in the center of a blue background. Beneath the seal is a gold-trimmed red banner with the words "State of Idaho." The state seal shows a female figure holding scales and a spear. They stand for justice and freedom. A male figure with a pick and shovel represents Idaho's mining industry. Between them are an elk's head and a forest scene. They stand for the state's wildlife and forests. At the top is a banner with the state motto, "Esto Perpetua."

MINING PRODUCTS

molybdenum, phosphate rock, sand and gravel, silver, lead

MANUFACTURED GOODS

computers and electronic equipment, food products, chemicals, wood products, machinery, paper

FARM PRODUCTS

sugar beets, potatoes, milk, wheat, sheep, beef cattle

PebbleGo Next Bonus!
To learn the lyrics to
the state song, go to
www.pebblegonext.com
and search keywords:

ID SONG

IDAHO TIMELINE

1620
The Pilgrims establish a colony in the New World in present-day Massachusetts.

1803
The United States buys the Louisiana Territory, including present-day Idaho, from France. The sale is called the Louisiana Purchase.

1805
Explorers Meriwether Lewis and William Clark become the first white people to explore the Idaho area. Shoshone and Nez Perce Indians help Lewis and Clark during their journey.

1809
Canadian explorer and fur trader David Thompson builds the first fur-trading post in Idaho. It is on the shores of Lake Pend Oreille in northern Idaho.

1834 Fort Hall opens as a trading post in southeastern Idaho. Fort Boise opens as a trading post on Idaho's western border.

1860 Gold is discovered at Orofino Creek in north-central Idaho. Mormons found Idaho's first permanent settlement in Franklin in southeastern Idaho.

1861–1865 The Union and the Confederacy fight the Civil War.

1863 Idaho Territory is created by the U.S. Congress. White settlers and American Indians continue to clash as settlers move onto Indian land. On January 29 Colonel Patrick Conner of the Union Army leads troops on an attack of Shoshone Indians. More than 200 Shoshone Indians are killed on the banks of the Bear River in southeastern Idaho. Fourteen soldiers are killed. The attack is called the Bear River Massacre.

1877 U.S. troops defeat the Nez Perce Indians in the Nez Perce War. The war takes place in Idaho, Oregon, Wyoming, and Montana as Indians fight to keep their land.

1890 Idaho becomes the 43rd U.S. state on July 3.

1914 Moses Alexander, a former mayor of Boise, is elected governor, becoming the nation's first Jewish governor.

1914–1918 World War I is fought; the United States enters the war in 1917.

1939–1945 World War II is fought; the United States enters the war in 1941.

1951 Near Idaho Falls, electricity is produced from nuclear energy for the first time ever.

1959 Brownlee Dam, which will produce electric power for the state, is completed on the Snake River.

1976 The Teton Dam on the Teton River in eastern Idaho bursts, flooding several towns, killing 11 people, and damaging more than $400 million worth of property.

1990 Idahoans celebrate the 100th birthday of their state.

2011 Idaho Governor C. L. "Butch" Otter issues a statewide disaster declaration after flooding in northern and southeastern Idaho.

2015 The Idaho giant salamander becomes the state's official amphibian; the measure is passed after five years of lobbying from a Boise eighth grader.

Glossary

ancestry *(AN-sess-tree)*—members of your family who lived long ago, usually before your grandparents

descendant *(di-SEN-duhnt)*—your descendants are your children, their children, and so on into the future

ethnicity *(ETH-niss-ih-tee)*—a group of people who share the same physical features, beliefs, and backgrounds

executive *(ig-ZE-kyuh-tiv)*—the branch of government that makes sure laws are followed

industry *(IN-duh-stree)*—a business which produces a product or provides a service

legislature *(LEJ-iss-lay-chur)*—a group of elected officials who have the power to make or change laws for a country or state

permanent *(PUR-muh-nuhnt)*—lasting for a long time or forever

plain *(PLANE)*—a large, flat area of land

region *(REE-juhn)*—a large area

sea level *(SEE LEV-uhl)*—the average level of the surface of the ocean, used as a starting point from which to measure the height or depth of any place

tourism *(TOOR-i-zuhm)*—the business of taking care of visitors to a country or place

Read More

Edgar, Sherra G. *What's Great About Idaho?* Our Great States. Minneapolis: Lerner Publications, 2016.

Ganeri, Anita. *United States of America: A Benjamin Blog and His Inquisitive Dog Guide.* Country Guides. Chicago: Heinemann Raintree, 2015.

Sanders, Doug. *Idaho.* It's My State! New York: Cavendish Square Publishing, 2014.

Internet Sites

FactHound offers a safe, fun way to find Internet sites related to this book. All of the sites on FactHound have been researched by our staff.

Here's all you do:

Visit *www.facthound.com*

Type in this code: 9781515703983

 Check out projects, games and lots more at
www.capstonekids.com

Critical Thinking Using the Common Core

1. What percentage of Idaho's agriculture is livestock? (Key Ideas and Details)

2. Would you like to live in Idaho? Use the text to support your answer. (Integration of Knowledge and Ideas)

3. The legislature is part of the executive branch of the government. What is the legislature? Use the glossary for help! (Craft and Structure)

Index